I CAN READ ABOUT

SHARKS

Written by C. J. Naden

Illustrated by Herb Mott

Troll Associates

10   9   8   7   6   5   4   3   2

SHARK!
The word makes people shudder.
A shark will attack anything —
small fish, big fish, people,
and even boats.

Is the shark really so dangerous?
What do we know about this creature?

We know the shark is a meat-eating fish.
It eats live or dead sea animals, and almost anything else.
Some strange things have been found in the stomachs of sharks—
everything from old junk to giant turtles.

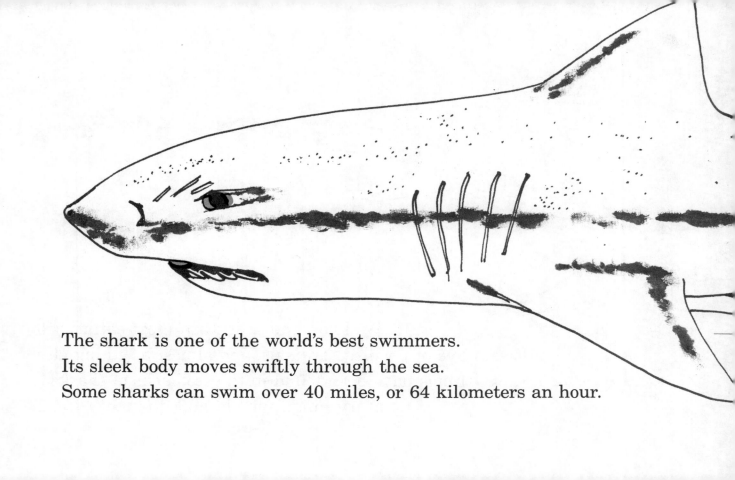

The shark is one of the world's best swimmers.
Its sleek body moves swiftly through the sea.
Some sharks can swim over 40 miles, or 64 kilometers an hour.

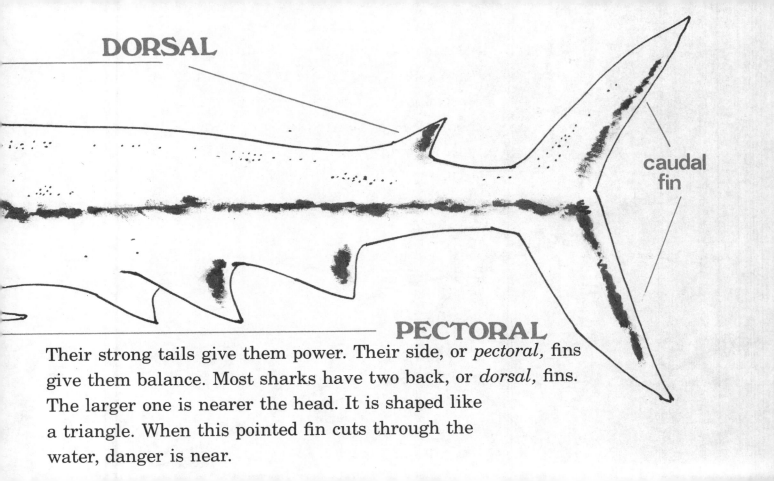

DORSAL

caudal
fin

PECTORAL

Their strong tails give them power. Their side, or *pectoral*, fins
give them balance. Most sharks have two back, or *dorsal*, fins.
The larger one is nearer the head. It is shaped like
a triangle. When this pointed fin cuts through the
water, danger is near.

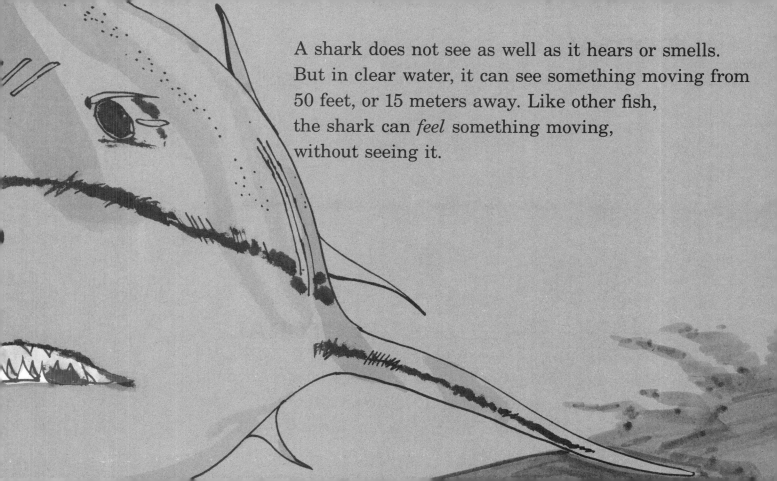

A shark does not see as well as it hears or smells.
But in clear water, it can see something moving from
50 feet, or 15 meters away. Like other fish,
the shark can *feel* something moving,
without seeing it.

Sharks are not considered very smart. But they have a keen sense of smell, and they hear well. These senses — plus their swimming speed — make them very good hunters and dangerous killers.

JAWS!
The shark has huge jaws and sharp teeth.
The jaws of the white shark are so strong that they can bite a person in half. Shark teeth grow in many rows. And the shark doesn't have to worry about losing a tooth. Another just moves up to replace it!

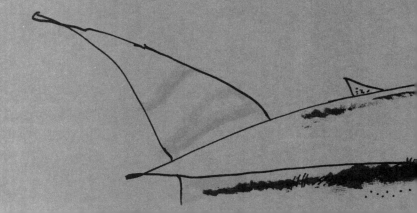

The shark is a fish,
but it is different from
most fish in many ways.
The shark has rough skin.
Its skin is tough and is covered
with what looks like very tiny teeth.
Sharkskin feels like sandpaper.

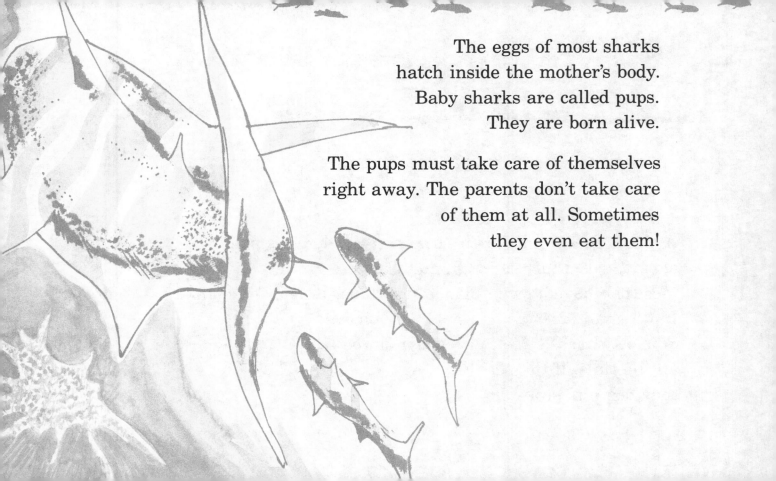

The eggs of most sharks
hatch inside the mother's body.
Baby sharks are called pups.
They are born alive.

The pups must take care of themselves
right away. The parents don't take care
of them at all. Sometimes
they even eat them!

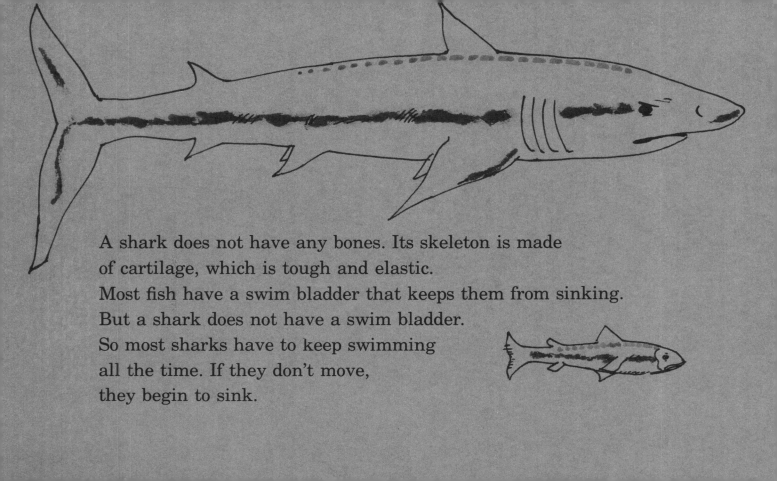

A shark does not have any bones. Its skeleton is made
of cartilage, which is tough and elastic.
Most fish have a swim bladder that keeps them from sinking.
But a shark does not have a swim bladder.
So most sharks have to keep swimming
all the time. If they don't move,
they begin to sink.

Like other fish, a shark breathes through its gills.
The gills of the shark are slits on each side of its head.
Most fish can pump water over their gills to get oxygen.
But most sharks cannot do this. Instead, a shark swims
with its mouth slightly open. Water flows into its mouth
and then out through its gills, taking in oxygen.
So most sharks have to keep swimming
in order to breathe.

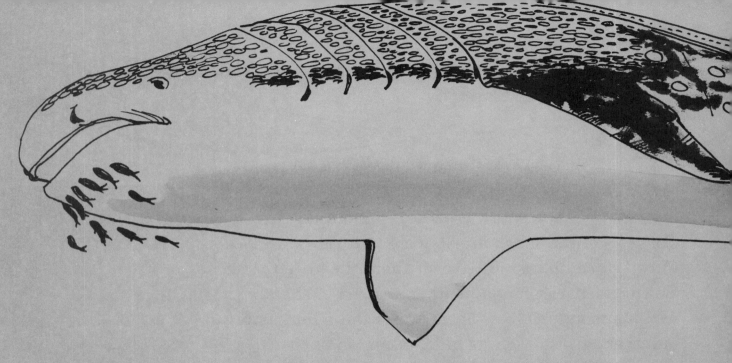

We know many things about sharks. But there are many things
we do not know. We do not know exactly how many kinds of sharks
there are. Scientists say there are at least 250 different kinds.

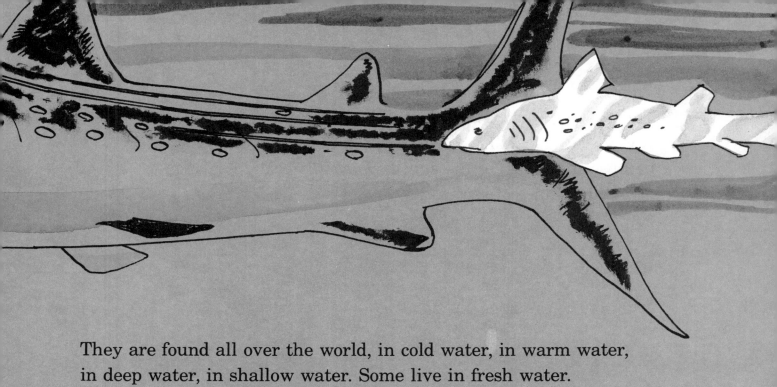

They are found all over the world, in cold water, in warm water, in deep water, in shallow water. Some live in fresh water. Some sharks weigh many tons. Some are less than a foot, or 30 centimeters in length.

There are different kinds of sharks.
The *basking shark* is the second largest kind of shark.
It can grow to about 40 feet, or 12 meters. It gets its name
because it "basks" in the sun. It warms itself by floating
near the surface of the water.

The basking shark lives in cool waters.
Despite its fierce looks, it eats only tiny plants and animals
called plankton. The other fish can swim by safely.

The *blue shark* gets its name from the color of its skin.
It grows to about 12 feet, or well over 3 meters.
This shark often follows ships for food thrown overboard.
The blue shark eats fish mostly. But people should stay out of its way!

The *bull shark* often lives in fresh water.
It is known to attack swimmers.
The bull shark grows to about 11 feet, or over 3 meters long.

The *hammerhead shark*
is found in all oceans.
It is the strangest-looking
member of the shark family. It grows
to about 15 feet, or 4.6 meters. The hammerhead
is very dangerous, and it is often found close to shore.
Its flat head looks like a hammer, with eyes and nostrils at each end.

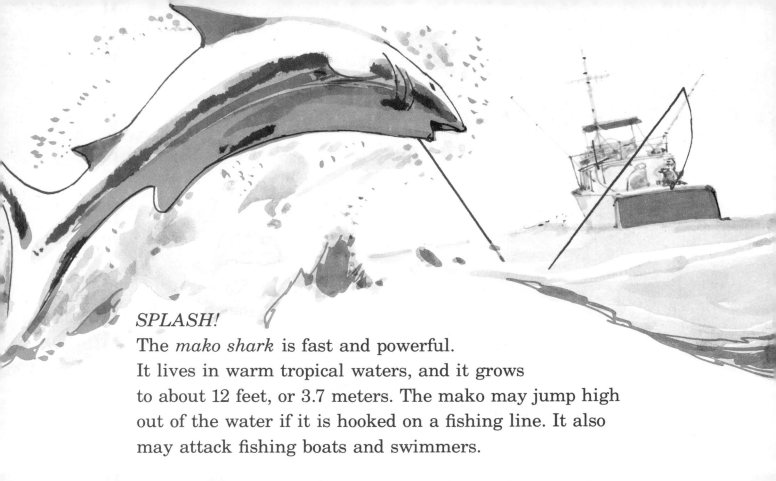

SPLASH!
The *mako shark* is fast and powerful.
It lives in warm tropical waters, and it grows
to about 12 feet, or 3.7 meters. The mako may jump high
out of the water if it is hooked on a fishing line. It also
may attack fishing boats and swimmers.

The slow-moving *nurse shark* will attack people if they get in its way. It grows to about 14 feet, or 4 meters. It is yellow brown or gray brown in color. This shark can pump water over its gills. So it does not have to swim all the time. Sometimes the nurse shark just lies quietly on the sea bottom. It is fond of crabs and lobsters.

The *thresher shark* grows to about 20 feet,
or 6 meters. But half of its body is tail.
This subtropical shark swims near the surface.
As far as we know, it does not attack people.

The largest fish in the world is the *whale shark*. It can grow to 60 feet, or 18 meters long. It can weigh more than an elephant.

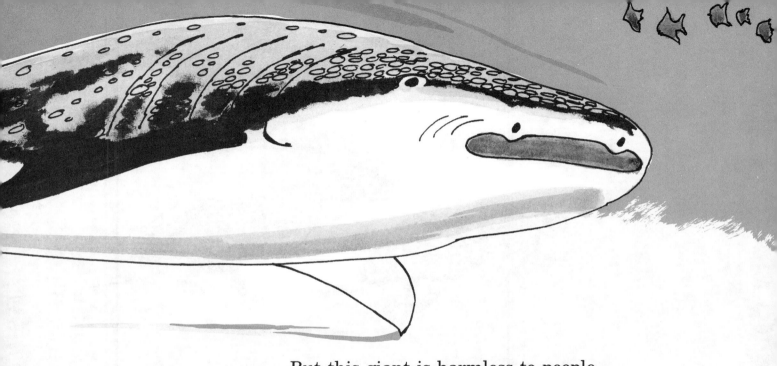

But this giant is harmless to people.
It eats only plankton and small fish.

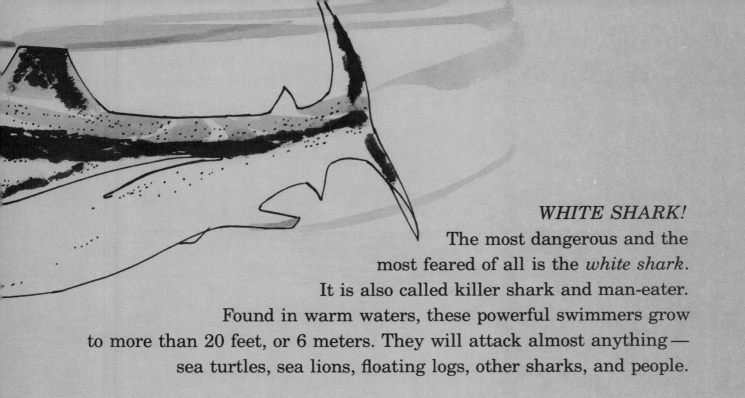

WHITE SHARK!
The most dangerous and the
most feared of all is the *white shark*.
It is also called killer shark and man-eater.
Found in warm waters, these powerful swimmers grow
to more than 20 feet, or 6 meters. They will attack almost anything —
sea turtles, sea lions, floating logs, other sharks, and people.

It is always big news
when a shark attacks a person.
But sharks do not attack often.
And only about 25 different types of
sharks are known to attack humans at all.

Feared and hunted, the shark has survived in the sea for millions
of years. It is, in fact, a prehistoric monster. Sharks of today look
and act like sharks that swam the oceans more than 100 million years ago.
Sharks have what they need to survive. They have a good body shape
for fast swimming. They have a good sense of smell for hearing and for
finding food. They have strong jaws and teeth for tearing food.

Why do sharks attack moving objects? Is it because they are hungry? Are they frightened? Scientists have been studying sharks for a long time, and they are still not sure.

Scientists have tried all kinds of things to stop shark attacks. They have spread different chemicals in the water to keep sharks away. But so far, there is no one thing that works all the time with all sharks.

Scientists would also like to know why
sharks have a *feeding frenzy*. Sometimes when they are eating,
sharks become very excited. With each bite, they get more excited.
Soon the sharks will eat or bite at anything in their way—boats,
rubber tires, logs, anything at all. A shark is especially dangerous
during a feeding frenzy. But scientists do not know why it starts
or what it means.

To learn about sharks, scientists must get close to them.

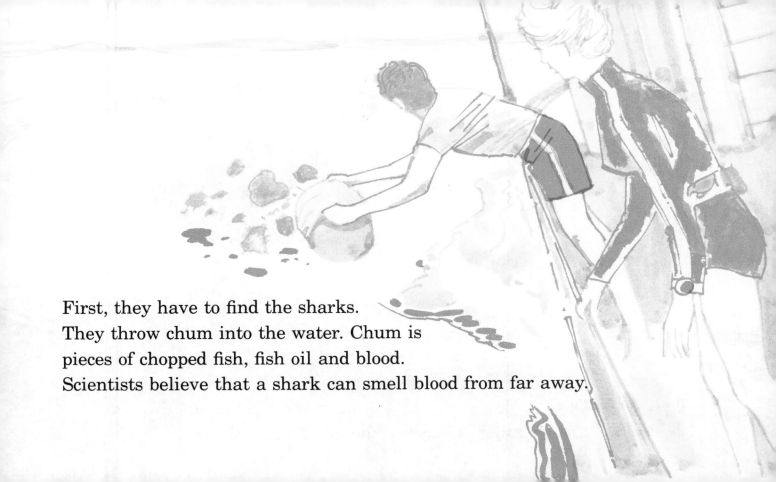

First, they have to find the sharks.
They throw chum into the water. Chum is
pieces of chopped fish, fish oil and blood.
Scientists believe that a shark can smell blood from far away.

They wait. Then, off in the distance, a huge pointed fin cuts through the water. It is the killer of the sea, the great white shark.

Slowly, slowly it circles the boat. More chum is thrown into the water. Like a streak, the shark jumps to the surface. It snaps up 25 pounds of meat in one gulp.

Now it is time for the diver to go below the surface. The diver will study the shark and take pictures. The diver is lowered in a metal cage. But the cage will not protect the diver if the white shark attacks. Its jaws can crunch right through the metal. Its mouth can swallow the diver in one bite.

Here it comes!

The white shark has seen the diver in the cage.
What will it do? Will it attack?
Or will it swim silently away?

The shark slowly glides by the metal cage. Each second seems like a year to the diver. The shark keeps circling, slowly, around and around.

And then, attack! Suddenly, the shark charges the cage.
Its mouth is open, its rows of teeth bloody and bared.

The diver waits, helpless.
The great mouth comes nearer.
The powerful jaws will surely
crunch the metal bars in two.

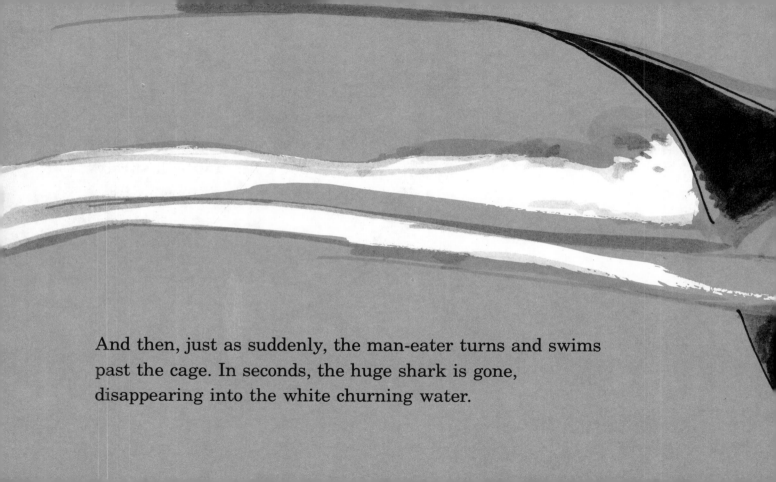

And then, just as suddenly, the man-eater turns and swims past the cage. In seconds, the huge shark is gone, disappearing into the white churning water.

What made the shark swim away? Why did it leave the diver alone?
We do not know. But the search for the answers goes on.
The diver is safe for another day and another dive.
There will be another chance to solve the mystery
of this strange creature of the sea.